PARENTING:
A SKILLS TRAINING MANUAL

Louise F. Guerney, Ph.D.

THIRD EDITION

Illustrations by

Joseph Fisher

in collaboration with

Bruce W. Guerney

Printed in the United States of America.

Library of Congress Cataloging in Publication Data.

Guerney, Louise Fisher
   Parenting: a skills training manual.

   1. Parenting.   2. Child development.   I. Title.
HQ772.G83   649'.1   78-70674
ISBN 0-932990-00-2

Table of Contents

PRACTICE SECTIONS

●●●●●●●●●●●●●●●●●

ALL OF THE PRACTICE SECTION PAGES ARE PER-
FORATED. THUS, IF THIS BOOK IS BEING USED AS A
MANUAL IN A PARENTING COURSE, THOSE PAGES
MAY BE TURNED IN TO THE INSTRUCTOR.

AN IMPORTANT MESSAGE FOR INSTRUCTORS

This publication is a revision and adaptation of *Foster Parent Training: A Manual for Parents*, published by The Pennsylvania State University, Center for Human Services Development, which was prepared by me as part of The Foster Parent Training Project, funded in part by the Pennsylvania Department of Public Welfare, Bureau of Children and Youth. Help with the writing of that manual was provided by research assistants, Carol Hatch and Andrew Sywulak; and Project Coordinators, Christine Deyss and Lenley Scheff. Of course, the *Foster Parent Training: A Manual for Parents*, should continue to be used for foster parent training.

Professionals or paraprofessionals interested in trainer's manuals, or in conducting training with either of the publications may contact the publisher or the author in care of the publisher.

The Parenting Skills Program Leaders Manual has been prepared by Louise Guerney for parent educators to enhance their use of this program. It contains general skills training information for both group and individual skills-training formats. It also has detailed Lesson Outlines with special training issues for each lesson. Parent educators and professionals of all disciplines who use this program will find the information invaluable. It can be ordered from IDEALS, at the address on the back of the cover page.

University Park, PA 16802   Louise Guerney
1988

vii

INTRODUCTION

The five skills for parenting which you will read in this book form a *system* for dealing with children. This is important to remember as you become acquainted with each skill. Each skill must be learned separately in order to best master it, but no single skill is considered enough for all situations.

For example, the first skill, Showing Understanding, is the sensible place to begin to achieve what you desire. The next step in most situations is to let your children know where *you* stand. These two skills increase understanding between you and your children. The system then provides three skills to help you to get cooperation from your children and to teach them how to behave, so that you and they both are satisfied. The final section of the book helps you sort out your priorities so that you can decide what aspects of situations are most important in order to select the best skills for any parenting situation.

It is the system as a whole which permits you to better communicate with your child, to solve behavior problems and conflicts, to teach your child proper habits and social behavior, and to increase self-esteem, confidence, and harmony for both of you.

1
WHAT PARENTS CAN EXPECT OF CHILDREN

All children are different, but all children go through certain stages of growth and development, although not necessarily in exactly the same way or at the same ages. By understanding how your child's behaviors relate to stages in the development of all children, you can know better how to handle things with your child. Below is an example of how this works.

Example:

If a tiny baby, say ten weeks old, catches hold of your hair, you probably would just take the child's hand away. You would know that you could not tell the baby to stop, because a baby at that age is not able to understand words. You would not yell, because it would do no more than upset the baby; the baby would not know what was going on.

At the age of one year, if the baby pulled your

(Example continued on next page)

Example: (Continued)

hair, you would tell the baby to stop, that it hurt, and perhaps remove the child's hand, but you would know that by this age the child would soon get the idea that you didn't want hair to be pulled.

At age three, the same child might get angry with her sister and pull her sister's hair. Now, you don't have to try to teach the child that pulling hair hurts; you understand that she has learned that pulling hair hurts. So you tell the child to stop, and you talk with her about not fighting. The same behavior is very different to others depending on the child's age.

IS THE CHILD READY TO LEARN?

A child's behavior and ability to live up to what you expect depend on two things:

1) the child's physical and mental readiness to do what you want.

2) the training the child has had in relation to what you expect now.

Some of the problems that parents have come from not knowing enough about the child's readiness to act in certain ways. This means that how well a child learns things may not be completely under your control or even under your child's control. No matter how much training you do or how hard your child tries, you will not be able to get your child to do things the child is not ready to do.

Examples:

A two year old child cannot ride a two-wheel bike no matter how much she thinks it would be fun to learn, or no matter how much effort you put into helping the child learn. Two-year-olds do not have the balance or coordination to learn. At four, the child can ride very well with training wheels. By age seven, hardly any children need training wheels for very long if the bike is the right size. Riding the biggest bike will come along a little later.

Whether or not they have eaten a lot of vegetables or brushed their teeth, most children will start to get their second teeth by the age of six.

Nearly all two-and-a-half-year-olds will go through a stage of saying "no," regardless of how they have been raised.

Teachers find that sixth graders often don't get notes home to parents because children at that age are absent-minded.

This doesn't mean that your child's learning is totally out of your control. Readiness and training are related. The secret is to time your training to the child's natural readiness. (You will find references in this chapter to later lessons in which parenting skills are discussed that can make it easier for you to train children in ways that are in keeping with their readiness.)

Examples:

When children show an interest in helping around the house, parents can encourage this by letting them help, praising them, and making it fun. On the other hand, parents can expect everything to be so perfect that the children give up helping unless they are forced to help.

When children are near walking age, parents play with them by standing them up, allowing them to let go, and to step toward them. This play helps children to practice so that they learn faster than if they were left to themselves. On the other hand, no amount of this game playing will get children to start walking if they are not yet physically able to support their own weight.

Keep what you expect of a child
in line with the child's age.

NEGATIVE TRAINING

The previous examples show how training can be more effective if it's begun when the child shows the first signs of the necessary physical and/or mental readiness. Sometimes, though, people or events in a child's life, beyond the parents' control, can affect the child in negative ways. Knowing about negative training can help parents, since much negative training comes about by accident.

Examples:

Around the age of three or four a child may stutter. Unless people draw attention to it, thereby training the child to worry about it, the stuttering stage will pass naturally. If the child becomes upset about stuttering because people try to correct it, the stuttering may become a fixed behavior.

Young children are usually very interested in their bodies, regardless of what others do. Being punished for this interest may only serve to fix too much importance on sexual matters for years to come.

Most six -year-olds are interested in but also very anxious about death and the supernatural. An experience with a death or a terrifying experience at a horror movie at this age will have longer lasting effects than they would later when this stage was already past.

ORDERLY GROWTH PATTERNS

The following sections (having to do with eating and sleeping habits, responsibility, etc.), are included because they relate to the concerns expressed by many parents. Age guidelines are given as to when the stages can be expected. These are *not* exact. Some children go through the stages much earlier or later than others. Some stages may be longer with some children and shorter with others. Perhaps it is best to think of these stages as the order in which growth takes place, rather than as a strict age schedule.

Example:

Every child will develop the muscle control to stand before developing the control to walk, and every child will learn to walk before learning to skate. But the ages at which children learn to do these things may be very different from child to child.

Children learn to talk before they learn to understand game rules. They must learn to understand the need for game rules before they learn to play by the rules. Individual children learn these things at different ages, but, again, all children follow much the same order in learning these skills.

By taking into account the *average* age at which a child may be expected to master the behaviors that follow, as well as thinking about those things which might slow down readiness, parents can avoid some of the problems of expecting too little or too much of their children.

EATING

Eating seems to be one of the most common concerns for parents. It includes several issues: table manners, appetite, and refusal of and preference for certain foods.

Table manners are very much related to children's ability to control their muscles (motor skill), control their energy, and to their ability to understand the value of good manners (social maturity). These skills develop over time as children gain experience and learn what is expected of them. People who watch many children grow in these abilities find that learning comes about more as a result of changes in readiness within the children than by strict teaching of what is proper.

About developing table manners

Young children first learn to handle a spoon, holding it, as they do everything, like a baby rattle. They master a fork next, but seldom can use a knife to spread before the age of five, or to cut before the age of eight. Graceful use of utensils is still developing at ten or even twelve years.

Young, healthy bodies have a lot of energy. At six or under, children wiggle around in their chair, grab food, spill things, stuff their mouths, talk a lot or loudly, or poke around in eating because of paying attention to other things. They quiet down a bit after age six, but continue to show excess energy by swinging their legs, etc. At eight they may show interest in eating and enter more quietly into dinner table conversations. After the age of eight they are more sensitive to manners and find it easier to control the urge to bolt away from the table before finishing the meal.

About appetite

Children's level of appetite is influenced by their interest in activities other than eating, which tends to make sitting down to meals less interesting for many. Using harsh measures to get a child to eat may turn eating into a terrible chore. A friendly atmosphere at the table will do more for making a healthy appetite than strict control and constant nagging.

A child's appetite is generally best at around age five or six. At two-and-a-half, it may be different from one meal to the next. Around seven years of age, different children will show different extremes—some having a very big appetite, while others never seem to eat much. By eight or nine, children eat more balanced meals according to their bodily needs. Breakfast is usually the meal in which children take the least interest.

About changing tastes for foods

Children normally go through stages of strong preference

for, or rejection of, particular foods. This may affect their appetites at any given meal. A child often refuses entirely to eat some foods.

At two years of age children begin to be "picky" about food and want some kinds again and again. At two-and-a-half, they like to say "no"—especially to foods like green vegetables. They will eat some things only if you feed them. At four, too, they are definite and consistent about likes and dislikes and want to eat a few foods all the time and not much else. Until the age of seven, children may continue to refuse certain foods, but after that age they may begin to try some different foods while still holding onto their favorites.

SLEEPING

Difficulties in getting children to sleep when they should and as much as they should are common. Nightmares and bed-wetting are also common.

About sleep and nightmares

By the age of five, most children need no more than an occasional afternoon nap and usually go to bed around 8:00 p.m. Some children may need music or story-telling to quiet them down so they can go to sleep, or they may need to stay up a bit later. Older children may settle down to sleep more easily if allowed to read before turning out the light.

Most children have trouble going to sleep at one time or another, but many children suffer from this difficulty much of the time. Putting the child to bed no earlier than his body requires, a light, soft music, or company in the room (for at least a short period) are all ways that can help the child fall asleep. Having a routine such as reading, talking, or quiet TV watching before bedtime may help. Exciting things near bedtime ought to be stopped if the child can't fall asleep. Even taking a bath can wind up some children.

At four-and-a-half, children begin to dream of wild animals or monsters. Nightmares are most frequent at five, and by age seven or eight begin to decrease. Some children may continue to have them until much older, especially if they have recently moved or been separated from their family.

About nighttime bladder control

Children's physical control over their bladders increases until the age of five. By that age, most children stay dry all night except for occasional accidents, but they may sometimes wake up and ask for help from a parent to go to the bathroom. By age seven most children seldom wet the bed.

HONESTY

Children are not naturally or automatically honest at all times. Understanding and controlling the impulse to lie, cheat, steal, or blame others is a developing ability. At one time or another, all children (and all adults) are not honest in one or more of the above ways. However, children will develop honesty and consideration for others if they are given training in keeping with their readiness. If the training is fair and not too harsh, and if they have not been forced into lying, cheating or stealing because they had no support for satisfying basic physical or emotional needs except by doing these things.

About developing honesty

As young as eighteen months, children may not admit blame for accidents because they are ashamed. At four they may admit their own fault, but may be dishonest by taking things from a store or school. The four-year-old seems to want everything. At this age it is difficult for the child to separate fact from fantasy. At five the child begins to more easily recognize the difference between the real and the make-believe. Blaming others for what the child has done is still typical. "Look what you made me do!" is a common statement. Five-year-olds may take something they value even when they know it's not theirs. Six-year-olds *might* not lie as much, but might cheat at games because they can't bear to lose. At seven, children generally lie less, but tattle on others.

Even older children tend to deny that they are to blame when you ask them about things. But by about nine they begin to be able to blame themselves, apologize, and be truthful, although they probably will have an excuse for

12

their actions. They can be very upset if blamed unfairly or punished too much. Likewise, they do not want to be praised too much—just a fair amount. If money or other things are not provided, they may try to get them dishonestly. At ten, conscience is growing, but is still not like that of an adult.

Having things they value can sometimes make children feel more like worthwhile people. If, for example, a child thinks a certain toy is very special, owning it may make the child feel special, too. Thus, it is hard for some children not to try to take things that don't belong to them.

Lying can also be a way of becoming "OK" if you're not sure you really are. Most children exaggerate a little (particularly at ages four and six) to try to become somebody to be pitied, or loved, or to seem worthwhile.

This isn't a sign of weak character, but of a desire to win necessary attention and approval—things we all value and try to get. Children must learn to feel that they are worthy of attention and approval without having to lie. Instead of saying, "Now Jimmy, you know it isn't true that your father plays for the Steelers, so why are you making it up," it might help to say something like, "Boy, you'd really like your dad to be a big important man." Responses like this should prove useful. You are not putting down the child's need, but at the same time you are letting the child know (in a nice way) that you recognize the exaggeration. Thus you are not encouraging the child to continue talking that way.

Since lying of this kind shows children's needs to feel better about themselves, you might also try to set up ways in which children can succeed and feel good about what they can do (see Structuring). You might also offer strong praise ("reinforcement") for positive behaviors when they occur.

RESPONSIBILITY

We expect children to become responsible in many different ways. All parents want to reach the point where their children see what work needs to be done, then pitch in on their own to do it. This is more than can be expected as routine behavior, but parents can come closer to this goal by taking their children's readiness for taking on responsibility into account.

Under responsibility we will consider obedience, helping, and chores—the major kinds of responsibilities parents want children to take.

About developing obedience

At about two-and-a-half children first start to be negative. At this young age, firm, calm action (rather than long or detailed discussion) usually gets the best cooperation. Ages three, five, and ten are likely to be more cooperative and obedient years. The years in between often are times when children try to assert their own importance, independence, and self-control in a variety of ways, often at the expense of immediate obedience. This is necessary for the development of self-esteem. Parents should not give in to all of the child's demands, but compromise is required in order not to interfere with the development of self-esteem.

At four, verbal restrictions work better than physical ones. The child's behavior may often seem out of bounds. Established routines and consistency will help with this.

At six the child tends to be verbally defiant. Indirect means of dealing with the child (see Structuring and Reinforcement) are more effective than arguing. Give children extra chances to obey, as if it were their own idea, since they often do the job later if you do not insist on *"instant"* obedience. One way to do this is by setting a time limit: For example, "Do it by the end of the TV show," or "by the next commercial." That helps them to get themselves together and you don't feel frustrated.

At seven children tend to be forgetful, slow to respond, inattentive, and easily distracted. Planning ahead helps here too.

At eight they tend to delay, but find reminders hard to

take. Often they are so sensitive about being "told" that they will respond to a word or a look. If you push more than that, they may be less cooperative. If you are pleasant, but firm, in communicating what is expected, you can help them control their behavior.

At nine they can keep themselves busy with their own activities, and may be slow to obey. They still should have clear instructions and a few reminders before you use consequences for failure to obey.

About cooperation with chores

Before children learn to do things for others, they should learn to do some things for themselves, such as feeding and dressing. Under the age of five, children like to help with simple tasks just to imitate or be near parents. At six, they enjoy responsibilities like setting the table and fetching things. At seven they may be able to cooperate by doing routine chores like cleaning up their rooms. Their attention may easily shift to something else before the job is done and they may need to be reminded several times to finish it.

At nine and ten, the beginnings of a truly cooperative attitude can be seen. Although his or her intentions to pitch in with the work are honest, the child is not good at following through, because other activities are more pleasant or rewarding. Setting up plans that are possible for children to carry out (see Structuring) may help them to be more reliable. Praise for a job well done (Reinforcement) may make children more willing to help, but just as they are still growing physically, they are still developing abilities to cooperate and be responsible and cannot be expected to be as dependable as adults should be.

SEPARATION

Up to five years of age, the mother is the center of the child's life. Her leaving, even briefly, causes some anxiety. Children cope with this anxiety well or poorly depending upon their age, previous experience, present state of mind, etc. If, for example, a child has just been in trouble, she may feel that her parent is leaving as a punishment to her even when this is not the case. Sometime around six years, however, children begin to take pride in being individuals, and brief separations can help develop independence and confidence even if they are still a bit anxious about it. Generally, the older the child, the less anxious he or she will be about being separated for a short time from his or her parents. Sometimes even teenage children experience some form of separation anxiety, like homesickness, if they are gone for more than an overnight trip.

Do *not* "sneak out" on small children to save them the anxiety of your parting. This may cause them to worry that you will disappear at some time when they're not looking, and they may become even more clinging and dependent. Letting them see you go and quickly return should in time overcome the problem for all but the smallest children. Very young children don't know the difference between ten minutes and "forever." Because of this, they may act like any separation is forever.

However, do not measure how much your children love you by how much carrying on they do when you leave. Some very young children, especially if they are with older brothers or sisters or familiar adults, *will* believe that you will be back soon and not fuss.

Small children protest or withdraw when they are upset about people leaving, so you can tell when they're upset. Older children may not be able to express their fears directly. They may cover up or deny their feelings, which may lead to troubles such as poor sleeping or bed-wetting.

Remembering the connection that often exists between these problems and fear of, or reactions to, separation, helps parents to cope better with their children. If parents become skillful in Showing Understanding (Lessons 2 and 3), the child may learn to express anxieties directly and overcome the need to do so by indirect means.

If parents have to go away from children, or have to leave them with relatives or in a hospital, even though they don't want to, the children may feel that they cannot count on adults to provide a stable situation for them. And true to the law saying "the burnt child dreads the fire" such children may not allow themselves to get close to other adults for fear of being let down again. They may treat even their parents strangely when they get back together again. This makes the parents feel rejected. Usually, this will pass after a long period of adjustment, particularly with younger children. Some older children will continue to mistrust adults by withdrawing, not showing affection, or by being rebellious or secretive in order to protect themselves from being hurt again. These are indirect expressions of separation anxiety. These behaviors may decrease with sensitive and skillful listening to children's feelings. (Or you might have older children write about their feelings). But if extreme anxiety about separation lasts for more than one year, you should get professional help.

SUMMARY

Children generally go through the same stages of growth and development, but not in exactly the same way or at the same ages. A child's ability to live up to what you expect depends on his stage of readiness as well as the training he has received. Many problems can be avoided if a parent waits until it seems clear that the child is ready before attempting to train or teach the child. Also, the work and strain for you in doing the training will be much less when the child is ready to learn. Examples of important growth patterns and stages of readiness should be considered, for example, in such areas as appetite, food preferences, table manners, nightmares, bladder control, honesty, obedience, responsibility, cooperation, and separation. In these areas, we pointed out in this chapter some things to watch for when it comes to teaching your child more grown-up ways of behaving.

●●●●●●●●●●●●●●●●●

Please turn now to Practice Section 1, page 121

2
SHOWING
UNDERSTANDING

Two sessions on showing understanding are included in your manual. Showing understanding is an important skill to use with children. It is a way of responding to things they tell you which, in turn, lets them know that you understand and accept how they feel.

You may have used this skill yourself, or perhaps other people have used it with you. If so, you can appreciate the difference between a response showing understanding and another kind of response, such as advice or sympathy. For example, if your father has just had a serious heart attack and your best friend says, "I know just how you feel," you may doubt that the friend really understands how you feel. If, however, your friend says "You are feeling very worried and upset," you would *know* that your friend does understand, and that may make you feel a little better.

The lessons include exercises and homework which will help you to master this important skill for use with your child.

What does Showing Understanding Mean?

Showing understanding is a special way of responding to children which communicates to them that you understand the feelings *behind* the messages they give you, as well as the messages themselves.

Why Should You Learn to Show Understanding?

1. Showing understanding helps your child to understand his own feelings and to learn how to cope with them. It helps him to build self-confidence by increasing his ability to solve his own problems. Children are more likely to follow through on solutions they arrive at themselves.

2. Showing understanding helps to build your child's trust and confidence in you. If, for example, your child knows that it's OK to tell you she's angry, she will have less need to throw a temper tantrum. Children are more likely to communicate openly and directly with you when they trust you. They do not need to use round-about ways to get their feelings out.

3. Showing understanding helps to promote a warm relationship between parents and children. In addition to helping the children deal with their own feelings, it will increase their willingness to respect your feelings and ideas.

4. Accepting a child's feelings is so powerful a method that it can often help children see things more clearly and, therefore, they are able to solve things themselves

without your having to tell them what to do or how to do it.

Why Does Showing Understanding Work?

Children talk to their parents daily about their ideas, problems, experiences, and feelings. This talking is an important part of their growth. Keep in mind that children are experiencing many things for the *first time* and may be trying to learn for themselves how to handle them. A parent's willingness to listen to a child, without giving advice and telling her how she *should* feel, can play an important part in the development of a child's confidence and self-esteem. Showing your acceptance means making a real effort to understand and care about what a child is saying. It also involves communicating this care and understanding to the child so that she knows you are trying to accept what she says *whether you agree with her or not.* This doesn't mean that you must go along with everything children say or do, only that you *first* show them that you understand their feelings.

Example:

A child, age 5, kicks her blocks on the floor, saying: "I hate these blocks. I can't pile them up right."

(Example continued on next page)

Example: (Continued)

Your response: "You're really mad because you can't build what you want."

This shows the child you know and accept how she feels. (It does not mean that you think kicking is good.)

Not this: "Oh, come on. You don't really hate your blocks."

You may mean to help the child with this response, but really you are telling her that you do not feel she should be angry. Trying to chase away the child's feelings can lead to worse feelings later on, even if for the moment it looks like things are working out OK.

DO's

1. You must *want* to listen to the child. If you can't listen at a particular time, wait until you can. You can't pretend to be a good listener.

2. You must work to see the world through the child's eyes, remembering that his feelings are just as real to him as yours are to you.

3. You must remember that feelings can change from one minute to the next.

4. You must trust the child's growing ability to handle his feelings and find his own solutions to problems.

Example:

In order to make some needed money, you baby-sit two children. One of them is an unpleasant child who gives your own son, age 7, a hard time. One morning before the children arrive, your son tells you that he's going to leave home if Michael comes and stays that day.

You have some pretty strong feelings about all of this yourself. You feel sorry that Michael is so mean to your son. On the other hand, you want him to try to get along with Michael, you need the money, and you can't cancel at this time.

However, in such a crisis, your first and foremost thoughts must be for *your son's feelings* and helping him to handle them. Remember you can best help him by responding to him—with understanding. It would not be helpful to say, "Well, go right ahead; Michael has to come here," or "I don't want to hear you talking like that. How would you feel if Michael's

(Example continued on next page)

---

mother heard you?" In both instances, you are not showing you care about him, which could make matters worse.

It would be a great deal better to say, "You just don't feel like you can put up with Michael much longer. You really want me to know that." This would open the door to further conversation, and maybe a little crying that would relieve his tension. Very likely a discussion will lead to his thinking of some ways to cope with Michael, once he's had a chance to talk it out.

Here is an example of how the conversation could go if you were to use the skill of showing understanding.

Example:

Son: I don't want to have to let Michael play here anymore. If he comes today, I'm going to go away somewhere and never come back.

Parent: You just don't feel that you can put up with Michael much longer. You want me to know that.

Son: Yes. He takes all my things and breaks up a lot

(Example continued on next page)

Example: (Continued)

of them.

Parent: It makes you feel really bad when he does these mean things to you.

Son: Yeah, and then you make me give him more stuff and share all the time.

Parent: It's hard enough on you with Michael but then I make it worse.

Son: You do. You don't listen to me — just him.

Parent: You wish I would pay attention to what you want too.

Son: Yeah (cries).

Parent: (holding his hand) You're feeling awfully bad about this.

Son: (stops crying) How about if I just put some of my stuff out and you keep the things I don't want him to break up in your room where he doesn't go.

Parent: You have an idea to stop him.

Son: Yeah. Can we do it that way, Mom?

Parent: You hope I'll say yes. And I will help you by putting away what you want. But I'll keep the things in the attic instead, where you can get them yourself.

In the above discussion, the parent did not try to judge the child's feelings or even mention the child's threat. The parent knows that the threat was a way of making sure she listened. The parent responded to that part in her first response, where she said, "you want me to know that." Had the parent preached about the evils of going from home or making threats, probably little would have gotten settled and, in all likelihood, the day would have been a bad one for the two boys (and the parent). Instead, the parent wisely gave most attention to the child's sadness and hopelessness. Once the son saw that she really listened and cared, and after a little chance to cry out his sadness, the child himself was able to make a suggestion.

Finally, note that it was only *after* listening to the child and *after* the child had asked her for an answer that the parent made a suggestion to the child about the place to keep the toys).

DON'TS

1. Don't criticize the child.

Example: It's stupid to think that nobody likes you.

---

2. Don't reassure or sympathize with the child.

Example: Don't worry, you'll find somebody to be your friend.

---

3. Don't attempt to solve the child's problem for him.

Example: Why don't you go ask Billy to play with you this afternoon?

---

4. Don't tell the child what to do.

Example: If you were nicer and would share your toys, the other kids would like you better.

---

5. Don't threaten the child with punishment for having negative feelings.

> *Example:* If you don't stop moping around the house and find someone to play with, you'll go to your room for the rest of the day.

6. Don't put down the child's feelings no matter how different they may be from your own. Your child will think you don't understand him if you tell him how he *should* feel.

> *Example:* Stop feeling sorry for yourself. You should be glad that the kids play with you most of the time.

Many of the Don'ts are considered to be helpful by parents, who often use them with the best intentions. However, it is often the case that children can be helped to solve problems on their own when they are listened to.

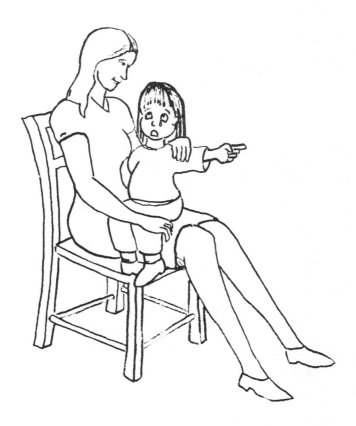

Listen to your child.

Greg's father is giving advice and criticizing Greg. He is not trying to understand Greg's problem and why he is upset.

In the last game I missed a fly ball and we lost the game."

Father: "You were really upset about missing that ball."

Greg: "Sure. It cost the game. I don't think they even want me on the team anymore.

Father: "You're afraid they don't want you to play because of that mistake."

Greg: "Well, I'm not the only one on the team who makes mistakes."

Father: "You know that other boys stay on the team who have made mistakes."

Greg: "Well, maybe I can give it one more try. I can't get any worse."

In this way Greg's father has recognized his son's feelings and helped him to see that he can handle those feelings himself without advice, instruction, or criticism from his parents. Greg even arrived on his own at the same course of action his father would have suggested. This might not always happen, but at the very least the child has an opportunity to get things off his chest.

Several steps are involved in learning to use skills that show understanding. The following exercises will help you to master these steps.

Exercise 1

Using the list of words on the left, choose the words you think best describe the child's feelings.

Example:

Your child is having trouble completing her homework. She drops her pencil and says, "I hate school. I never want to go there again."

The child is feeling *frustrated, angry, bothered.*

Feeling Words:	Situations:

Feeling Words:

frustrated

angry

happy

guilty

proud

frightened

embarrassed

resentful

pleased

sad

affectionate

worried

bothered

tired

bored

Situations:

1: Your child comes home from school with a good report card. He hands it to you and says, "Hey, look at this!"

He is feeling ———————————— .

2: Peggy, 8, is complaining about a chore she has to do. She refers to her brother Tom, 6, saying, "Why doesn't he ever have to do anything around here?"

She is feeling ———————————— .

3: Paul makes a home run in the Little League game. He asks after the game, "Well, did you see me? What did you think?"

He is feeling ———————————— .

Choose the best *response* to the child.

Example:

Jenny is having a hard time learning her piano lesson. She says, "Oh, I just can't do this right at all."

Below, response b is the best response.

a) Come on, Jenny, you can't quit now.

b) You're really trying, but you just can't seem to get it right.

c) That's OK, just keep practicing and it'll come to you.

Exercise

Elaine, age 12, says, "I don't know why I can't wear eye shadow to school. Everybody else does."

Choose the best response:

a) Everybody else does *not* wear eye shadow to school and you know it.

b) You really want us to let you wear eye shadow to school.

c) School is no place for eye shadow, especially at your age.*

* Choice "b," "You really . . . " is best.

Exercise 3

In this exercise you are to choose the *worst* response for each situation.

Example:

Tom, age 9, says, "Nobody likes me. I'm going to run away."

Below response c is the *worst* response.

a) Tom, you know we love you and want you to stay with us.

b) You feel troubled, and you hate the way you're treated here.

c) Tom, you be quiet or go to your room.

Exercise:

Carol, age 6, is trying to ride a two-wheel bike. She comes in crying, saying, "I wish I'd never got that bike. I keep falling off and I'll never learn to ride it."

a) You poor thing, look at that scraped knee!

b) Get back outside right now and try again.

c) It looks like you're having some sad time with your bike. It's got you down.*

*Choice "b," "get back outside. . ." is the worst response.

SUMMARY

Showing understanding can build children's confidence in themselves and can increase their respect for you. If you help children to communicate honestly with you by showing that you understand their feelings, you open the way for building a more satisfying relationship between you and your children, and for helping them solve their own problems.

●●●●●●●●●●●●●●●

Please turn now to Practice Section 2, p. 123

3
SHOWING UNDERSTANDING

PART TWO

You have learned the basics of showing understanding in the last lesson. This lesson is a review which will provide you with further practice in the skill of showing understanding and it introduces some new situations which parents frequently run into. They require you to put aside your own feelings in the situation before responding to the child's feelings, dealing with your own feelings later.

Remember that the most important factor involved in showing more understanding is to try to see things as children see them. You can "accept," that is understand and respect, someone's views or feelings even if you disagree with them or don't think they are justified. If children know that you do accept and understand their feelings, even when you don't agree with them, they will gain confidence in you and in themselves. They will pick up some of your accepting ways. Your respect for them will make it easier for them to show the same respect for you and others.

Children and adults alike are much more likely to behave in appropriate ways when their feelings are understood. You don't have to go along with everything your child says or does. *After* you have accepted his feelings, you can suggest alternatives or place limits if necessary. However, accepting the child's feelings can help to get to problems while they are small, before they become big ones. Even with adults, dealing with feelings can help with problems.

Example:

You are mad at yourself for having said you'd do some work for a group you belong to because you found out that many others are not helping at all. Also, you have not been feeling well.

(Example continued on next page)

Example: (Continued)

When you mention this to a friend, she says, "Yeah, you feel bad when people just keep expecting from you." As a result of this accepting statement, you go on further to tell about not feeling appreciated. After this talk, you do the work without feeling a grudge. And, at the next meeting, you suggest an idea yourself on how to get more people to work which everyone likes.

BUT...

Example:

If your friend had said, "So why do you keep volunteering, stupid? You know they're like that," you'd be so busy defending yourself against this statement, you'd probably not be able to sort out your feelings or think of constructive suggestions yourself.

Conclusion: Expression and acceptance of feelings tends to result in more constructive ways of dealing with problems.

You have strong feelings that he shouldn't hit anyone to get what he wants. But keep in mind that you want Timmy himself to see that he doesn't need to resort to hitting to solve problems. An immediate reply like, "Don't you ever hit anybody!" prevents discussion which *could* lead Timmy to understand, on his own, that he did the wrong thing. Instead, a statement like, "You didn't really want to hit him, but he made you angry by taking your truck" shows Timmy that you understand his feelings. He won't need to defend himself against suggestions of other ways to deal with children who take his toys. These would fall on deaf ears until the air has been cleared.

In other words, it's all right to offer suggestions of solutions to problems *after* you've recognized the child's viewpoint by reflecting his feelings. *It's also important to remember that when you finally do offer help, you should not be critical of the child or deny the feelings you've just accepted.* You are not accepting feelings only to get to your own suggestions. You are understanding and accepting the child's viewpoint, and going on from there.

Example:

You undo your original, accepting response by adding a statement that does not *accept* where the child is, that is, the child's viewpoint.

"You really didn't want to hit him, but he made you angry by taking your truck. *Of course, if you didn't get mad so easily, you wouldn't even think of hitting.*"

This immediately puts the child on the defensive, making him less able to find possible solutions. A better way of handling the situation could be:

Example:

Adult: "You really didn't want to hit him, but he made you angry by taking your truck."

Timmy: "Yeah, I was really mad."

Adult: "I can see why that would make you mad, but I don't like to see you hitting other children. Next time Paul does something like that it might help if you told him you were angry and wanted your truck back. If that doesn't work, maybe you could ask me or another adult to talk about the problem with you and Paul."

●●●●●●●●●●●●●●●●

Please turn now to Practice Section 3, p. 125

44

4

PARENT MESSAGES

You have learned how to listen to your child and how to understand and respond to his or her point of view. Sending parent messages is a skill which helps you to express *your feelings to the child* about his actions, especially troublesome ones. Positive parent messages should be used freely, too. Parent messages can communicate what makes you unhappy about the *child's behavior* without putting down the child himself. Parent messages allow you to tell a child that he is *doing something* which annoys you, without telling him that *he's* bad. Making your feelings clear to the child helps him know what you expect of him.

What are Parent Messages?

Parent messages tell your child how *you* feel about problems he makes for you and what he can do to help you out. You can also use parent messages to tell your child what he does that pleases you. (See "Reinforcement" chapter 6.)

It's important to let the child know your
point of view without putting her down.

How Do Parent Messages Work?

When your child does things that frustrate, disturb or annoy you, tell her clearly how her *actions* affect you rather than suggesting that there is something wrong with the child by criticizing *her*. Try as often as possible to accept her feelings before stating yours. Understanding should nearly always be your *first* response. A statement of your feelings can follow as a second response.

Example:

You are trying to rest. Your six-year-old is banging on a drum in the same room. Rather than saying, "Why do you always bother me when I'm trying to rest?", try, "I know you'd like to play your drum, but I'm getting very annoyed because I'm trying to rest and I can't if you make noise in here."

Notice the difference between the two statements. The first statement is a criticism of the child which says, in effect, "You are bad because you bother me." The second statement, however, tells the child how you feel about what she's doing without condemning her. By using a parent message, you let the child know how you feel about what she's doing and you give her a chance to change her actions on her own because she knows what kind of problem she's creating. A threatening or accusing response may make her feel angry and resentful. Anger and resentment make people of all ages feel less cooperative.

Exercise:

You are cooking dinner. Your child wants you to fix a broken toy. First reflect his desire to have the toy fixed. After that, which of the following would be the best parent message?

a) Don't bother me with that thing now. Come back later.
b) Can't you see I'm busy? Come back later.
c) I'm worried about getting dinner ready on time. I'll fix your toy after dinner.

The last message, above, is the best because you gave the child information about your point of view. A child can put up with waiting better when he knows your problem than if he is put off as though *he* was bad for asking. (Of course, you would want to do what you said you would later so that the child knows that it was your feeling at the moment that really was the problem and it was not a way of avoiding the issue.)

Remember these points when using parent messages:

1. Accept the child's feelings first.

Example:

"You'd like to climb all the way to the top."

---

2. State your feelings clearly.

Example:

"I am very *worried* and *afraid.*"

---

3. Give the child the reason for your feelings or state the problem.

Example:

"I am very worried when I see children going to the top of that tree. I am afraid they'll fall down and get hurt."

---

4. If you expect something of the child, state clearly what it is.

Example:

"It is important to me that you come down to the big strong branches."

---

5. Don't condemn or accuse the child in any way.

Example:

Don't say: "You should not scare me like that. You're mean to do that."

When you talk this way (sending parent messages), you recognize your own feelings of resentment, anger or frustration, and you tell the child how his actions affect you without saying that he is bad or at fault. Remember that there is a difference between telling a child that he is *doing* something which bothers you for some reason and telling the child that *he* is bad because he does it.

6. Don't lecture or threaten.

Example:

Four-year-old Kathleen wants to stay up past her bedtime. *Don't* say, "You'll get sick if you don't go to bed." Scare tactics like this can have bad effects. *Say instead,* "I need to spend some time with Mommy at night. It is the only time we have together. I want you to go to bed on time so that I can do that."

Exercise:

Your child leaves his bike in the driveway. Write a parent message which states your feelings about this without criticizing the child.

Your own feelings and needs are reason enough to make your child change the way he behaves. Once your child knows how you feel and what you expect of her, she will usually want to behave in a considerate way. It is not necessary to say things like, "Everybody else does things this way," or "You'll wind up in jail if you keep that up." This will be especially true if you are trying to respect her feelings and to show understanding.

Exercise:

Brian asks for a third piece of candy.

Choose the best response:

a) Brian, that candy will make you sick.

b) I don't want you to have more because I am worried about the cavities you are getting.

c) Don't be so greedy!*

* "I don't want . . . " (b) is best.

Although parent messages are often enough to cause children to behave the way you'd like, there are times when further action must be taken. (See lessons on Structuring and Setting Limits.) However, a parent message is always a good starting point because it helps the child understand your feelings and your reasons for them *before* you move on.

Example:

Your eight-year-old keeps interrupting a discussion you're having with your wife.

Say: I'm getting annoyed with all these interruptions because I need to talk to Mommy for a few minutes," (Parent Message.) "Run outside and play. I'll come get you when we're through and then we can talk." (Structuring.)

If the child refuses:
"I am very annoyed with all these interruptions. If you bother me again you'll have to go to your room until I can talk to you. (Limit.)

Positive Parent Messages

Sharing your positive feelings about your children is equally important to letting them know where you stand. If you let them know when they do something that pleases you, they will conclude "Parents like that" and may continue or increase the behaviors you compliment them about. (See Reinforcement).

Example:

Karen, age 6, has cleaned up the playroom without being told. A good parent message would be: "What a beautiful job you did cleaning this room. I'm so proud of you for helping out without my having to remind you." A warm hug could be added.

Everyone likes to be complimented for things they do well, because everyone likes to know that they can please others through their actions. Thanks, praise, and affection can go a long way toward helping all of us to be cooperative and considerate. Both words of affection and physical affection help children know we fell positive about them, even if they haven't done anything special but just because we love them.

Example:

Your friend Paul asks you to help him fix his car. You work on it for three hours on Saturday afternoon. When you're through working, he jumps into his car, saying that he must hurry to visit some friends. Since he didn't express any appreciation, you probably won't be anxious to help him again.

If, however, he says, "Gee, thanks for your help. You did a great job and I appreciate your taking all this time to help me out," you'd probably be willing to do him another favor in the future.

SUMMARY

Using parent messages to communicate your feelings to children will make them more willing to behave in appropriate ways. Parent messages let children know what you expect of them with less chance of making them feel angry or resentful than a "put-down" or a criticism would. Used along with showing understanding, parent messages help place respect for each other at the core of the family's relationships.

●●●●●●●●●●●●●●●●

Please turn now to Practice Section 4, p. 131

5
STRUCTURING

When you know beforehand that problems might come up with your child, you can take positive steps to prevent those problems. This kind of planning ahead to prevent problems is called *structuring*. The following lesson discusses situations in which problems often come up and lists some steps which you can take to eliminate or reduce those difficulties. Some of them are simple procedures which you may already be using, but having the procedures spelled out in detail here may help you to use them better.

What is Structuring?

Structuring means planning surroundings and events in a child's life so that he will be more likely to be able to fulfill your expectations and have his own needs met at the same time.

Why should you use structuring?

Structuring can help you to avoid problems. Children who enter a school bus one at a time, rather than pushing to crowd in all at once, are *structuring* their behavior. Realizing beforehand that pushing and shoving can lead to accidents or fights, the children structure their behavior by entering single file in order to prevent such things from happening.

By thinking ahead about the kinds of problems that might come up in a given situation, we can often take steps to eliminate or reduce those problems.

Example:

Most people keep poisons, knives, and medicine out of the reach of small children. This is a simple form of structuring the child's surroundings. It keeps you from having to punish the child for playing with dangerous things, and it prevents the child from hurting himself.

Structuring involves taking positive action to prevent or solve problems before having to resort to punishments or threats. Structuring involves the recognition of two principles: 1) that people (especially children first learning new behaviors) are *not* likely to do the right thing without some thinking ahead; and 2) that we can and should take steps to try to see that desired behaviors do occur.

Sometimes structuring the child's *environment* can prevent or reduce problems. Sometimes you may have to structure *events* in the child's life as well.

Structuring the Environment

Some ways in which we can structure the environment are:

1. Provide a variety of activities. Children get bored just like adults do. When they're bored, they're more likely to get into trouble or nag their parents for something to do. They might even do something wrong just to get attention. Provide children with toys and games that are suited to their age and interests, such as model airplanes, puzzles and bikes, or tinker toys, blocks, trucks, cars and dolls for young children.

2. Arrange the home for children. Houses and furnishings are built for grown-ups. Children are smaller and less skillful and therefore less able to do things properly which are easy for us. Some things you can do to make it easier for children to do the right thing are:

   a. Have a small stool for the child to use at the sink to make washing easier.
   b. Have a low place to hang clothes so the child *can* hang them up.
   c. Use plastic or paper cups instead of breakable glasses or cups.
   d. Put a fence around the yard which keeps children within sight and off the street, while still allowing them to go out on their own.

Help children by giving them a way to
do things at the right time and place.

Structuring encourages learning, independence, and responsibility. Children usually want to do the right thing and they gain self-confidence when they do. Thoughtful planning by parents can help children learn to do what you (and they) want.

Example:

A special play time in a special play area where he knows he won't be interrupted by you can help him to learn to respect your privacy when you need it.

Exercise:

Give an example of something you might do to structure the environment for a child.

Structuring Events

Structuring *events* in a child's life may be a little more difficult, but can be very helpful in avoiding or solving problems that may come up, as the next example shows. Two ways of dealing with the situation are described.

Example:

Bobby, 11, is too old for a baby sitter but not quite old enough for his parents to feel sure he can sit for himself and his younger sister. He wants to do so and they want to let him, but they think that everything must be straightened out beforehand.

Method 1.

This is how things might go if Bobby's parents structured the situation:

They look for a time when they will be gone for only a couple of hours at a place where they can be reached by phone. They tell Bobby to call after one hour to tell them how things are going. If Bobby doesn't call, they call him. Before leaving, sister is dressed for bed and a bedtime snack is provided. She is given a new book to interest her so that Bobby doesn't have to read to her, since reading sessions often turn into fights. They tell Bobby that when they get home they will have hot chocolate and cookies together. They do *not* say they will have this treat only if he does well. They assume he will do well and have made everything in the situation as easy as possible for him to succeed. Any little things Bobby may do wrong during the evening are ignored in honor of his having tried a new behavior and done the main thing well.

Method 2.

This is how it might have gone if the parents were not aware of the importance of structuring.

The next time the parents go out, they ask Bobby to sit. Before leaving, Bobby's mother says, "We really don't like this, but we're going to let you try it anyway. If it doesn't work out, you won't get another chance for a long time. Get your little sister ready for bed, fix her a snack and read to her. You be in bed by nine-thirty, and don't bother us unless it's an emergency." Bobby's father adds, "Tomorrow I'm going to check with your sister to see if you were good, and if you weren't, you'll be sorry."

Notice all the loopholes in Method 2 that *could* turn the situation into a failure for children *and* parents.

You must make sure when setting up a situation like asking a child to do a chore that he knows exactly what is expected of him. Don't assume that he will be able to do what you want just because you ask him to. Plan ahead and think about problems that could arise. Neglecting to structure such situations so that the child can succeed could lead to failure for him and annoyance for you.

Spelling things out and showing the child how to do things can eliminate some of the bickering over when and how a job should be done. It can prevent you from having to ask the child to do the job over again or to complain to him about the mess he made of it.

Example: (Continued)

and show him how to fill the sink with hot water and the proper amount of detergent. Tell him in what order to wash things (". . .glasses first, then dishes, then silverware, then pots and pans") and show him how to rinse and stack dishes in the dish drainer. Have paper towels handy so he can wipe up any spills. Do not fuss if he makes a little mess or gets a little mixed up.

You may run into some problems which seem more difficult to solve but which can at least be made less troublesome if you plan ahead.

Example 1:

Your child wants a dog. He begs you, saying he will care for it, clean up after it, and walk it every day. You are not so sure. Since the whole family will be affected by keeping a pet, you might all sit down together and discuss the situation before getting the dog. When the child is sick, for example, someone else will have to care for the pet. What arrangements can you make for the animal when you all go on vacation? Who else in the family will be willing to help care for the dog?

Example 2:

Your child has gotten a new bicycle. He should know when and where he can ride it and where he should keep it. It helps for you to express rules positively. Instead of saying, "Don't cross any streets on that bike," try drawing a map of the block, saying that he can ride all the way around it but nowhere else.

Example 3:

Your child is having trouble with her English lessons and is afraid to ask the teacher for help because she thinks the teacher will scold her. You plan ahead with her, deciding on how and when she could best approach her teacher for help. As practice, and just for fun, you could take the part of a "mean teacher" responding to a child asking for help, then a "nice teacher." This helps to relieve the child's stress and build her confidence. Having a clear picture in mind of how to approach difficult situations can be very helpful to a child learning to handle herself in the world.

Some situations may confuse or frighten a child, and he may need your advice and reassurance. A first trip to the dentist can be scary, but if you structure it beforehand by telling the child what is likely to happen at the dentist's in a *realistic* way, he may be less frightened and more willing to cooperate.

Exercise:

In one paragraph, write what you would say to a six-year-old child to get him ready to go to the dentist. Avoid unrealistic promises and avoid details which might frighten him. Build in something you could *do* to make it go well, e.g. taking a book for the child in case the dentist has only adult magazines.

Structuring will not eliminate all problems, but it can help you to eliminate some and make solving others a little easier.

Re-structuring

You can use the principles of structuring to stop behaviors that are already in progress as well as to keep them from starting. If you change the structure of a situation to stop unwanted behaviors, you are re-structuring. You would re-structure when you can see that given the same person, things, and time, that the unwanted behavior will continue.

Examples:

A child is finger-painting and there is no apron or other cover to put on her. You help set her up with crayons instead. If the child is old enough, use a parent message to explain.

A baby is trying to go up stairs that are too high for him. You take him away from the stairs, while you hand him a toy that you know he likes, or re-direct him to another safer place that you think will interest him.

As with structuring, the adult takes an active part in trying to stop unwanted behaviors. In re-structuring, the adult tries to redirect the child to a different thing, place, or activity in order to correct a problem. The adult does not expect the child to be able to handle this situation by himself. It is particularly useful for younger children for that reason. Of course, if the child does not stop in spite of your re-structuring efforts, setting a limit may be necessary. (See chapter 6, Limits.)

Examples:

This

Do give baby a rattle to shake if he is banging on a good table with a spoon.

Not this

Grab the spoon and take off with it, leaving baby upset and perhaps determined to get back the spoon.

This

Stop a fight between two young children for the same toy by bringing out some other similar toys. You are re-structuring by changing the number of toys for them to choose from.

Not this

Scold them or punish them in some other way or take the toy away from them without replace-

(Example continued on next page)

Example: (Continued)
ment. A parent message could be given here ex-
plaining that you don't like fighting and that finding
other toys is what you want them to do.

Re-structuring Exercises:

1. A four-year-old is trying to drink coffee from your
cup. You do not want him to drink coffee but realize
he wants to imitate you. Which of the following
would be the best way to re-structure?

   a) Tell him he is not allowed to drink coffee until
   he's older.

   b) Promise him some soda later in the evening.

   c) Give him a drink of cocoa in a cup like yours.*

2. Your 10 and 11-year-old daughters tell you they are
going to see a horror movie, which you feel sure will
greatly upset them. How might you re-structure
their time to avoid the movie yet meet their needs

* "Give him. . ." (c) is best.

for an interesting experience? Write your plan in the space below.

Points to remember about structuring, re-structuring:

1. Review situations where trouble has occurred and in new situations look ahead to see what problems might arise.

2. Decide how you want things to work out.

3. Think of ways to prevent or solve the problems.
    a) Have you thought of everything that could go wrong?
    b) Have you "built in" all the procedures or things that can make it turn out right?
    c) Do you need to discuss the plan or problem with the child?

4. Give clear instructions to the child about what he can expect and what you expect of him. Be consistent.

5. Have an alternative to your first structuring plan in case it doesn't go well.

6. If things go wrong even after you are convinced you've covered all "loop-holes" by structuring and re-structuring, impose limits and consequences (see Limits).

7. Praise the child when things go well.

8. Don't interfere with those things a child is doing for himself which don't affect you. For example, don't tell him how to color a picture or part his hair, unless of course, he asks you to. If you keep out of areas of activity where children can do things or decide things for themselves, they will be less likely to resent your structuring of other situations.

Structuring can help your child to feel responsible and encourage him to be independent. But when in doubt, it is always best to start out expecting that a child can do less rather than more. In this way, you won't be expecting the child to meet standards that are too big for him to handle. Starting easy, there is room for making improvements which encourage the child to try harder. Nothing "succeeds like success." Structuring sets things up so that children can practice, master, and be proud of doing the things we expect of them.

72

Example:

Your sister's daughter, age 7, must live with you for a few weeks while your sister is in the hospital. Since they live in another town, you are not sure how she feels about sleeping alone in the dark.

Do not jump to the conclusion that she will be able to do things in the grown up way. As we know, even mature and well-adjusted children have some "slow spots." Assume that she will want a light at night and leave it on. Let her *tell you* if she doesn't want it. This will save her embarrassment if she does need it. Later, when she feels more secure in this strange house, she may not need the light.

SUMMARY

Structuring and re-structuring are ways to avoid problems by thinking about what you want to happen and taking
positive steps to see that things come out the right way. By
planning ahead with your child, you make life easier for both
of you.

●●●●●●●●●●●●●●●●

Please turn now to Practice Section 5, p. 133

6
REINFORCEMENT

In the last lesson we discussed setting up situations in ways that enable the child to do things he needs to do without having things work out badly for you and for him. Once things are structured, you can help the child keep up his good behaviors by rewarding or *reinforcing* them. All of us like to have approval. If you let your child know by praising or rewarding him that you appreciate his good behaviors, he will be more likely to continue or increase them in order to please you, because the praise you give him will make him feel good about himself.

Approval

Reinforcement means that you give a child approval for something she has done that pleases you so that she will be more likely to continue to behave in ways of which you approve.

Why should you use reinforcement?

It is easier and more pleasant for both parents and children to live in an atmosphere of approval and reinforcement than in an atmosphere of disapproval and punishment. When you reinforce, that is, reward or approve of something children have done, you are telling them you like that particular behavior. Since children want approval and do not want punishment, they will continue or increase the kinds of behaviors which are rewarded.

By reinforcing a behavior you are helping children to learn to do the right thing on their own. After a time they will do (or not do) as desired on their own without your having to reinforce. The behavior will become second nature to them, part of their natural way of doing things. This is especially important, because no parent can be around to tell children what to do all the time.

It is important to realize that *all* behaviors are learned *only* when the learning of the behaviors has some reward value. Therefore, it is not bribing or rewarding for what "should be done anyway." Reinforcing is the better word to use because that is what results from using rewards or reinforcements. The behaviors are reinforced, that is, become stronger. What you are doing is putting the laws of learning to work *for you.* If you don't reinforce what is desirable, you run the risk that undesirable behaviors will hold greater rewards.

76

This diagram illustrates the happy circle created when a parent rewards a child.

Child acts "good"

Child is happy and
wants to please parent

Parent shows approval

Quite a different circle is created when a parent scolds or punishes the child most of the time. The child feels angry, upset, and unloved.

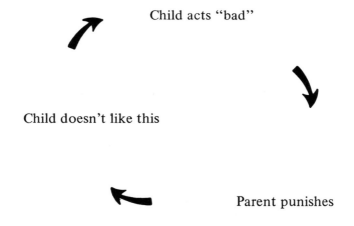

Child acts "bad"

Child doesn't like this

Parent punishes

How can you set up a circle of approval and reinforcement so that you can increase your child's good behaviors? Look for and begin to set up more opportunities to reward your child.

Exercise:

Make a list of behaviors you would like to see increased.

1.

2.

3.

4.

Now that you have this list, begin to look for times when your child behaves in these ways. Or, you could structure certain situations so that the child can behave as you'd like and give you the opportunity to praise or reward him. (See Structuring.)

Show him your approval by:
1. giving him your attention
2. admiring or praising him
3. giving him affection - hugs or kisses
4. giving him treats—a juice pop, a penny, a special privilege.

For example, if you want your children to play cooperatively with friends or brothers and sisters, look for times when they are playing nicely and reward them. You could say, "You children are really being nice. That's wonderful to see." Make your praise short and sweet. Do not go on and on —it can backfire if you overdo it. (A child can be overwhelmed by too much praise and begin to worry that he will not be able to "live up" to it.) Do not attach demanding statements like, "Now, be sure you play as nicely next time." (That would ruin your first positive statement.) Children will be pleased if you notice their good behavior and will be more likely to increase that behavior. The best policy is to use short statements of praise every time they apply. One long testimonial to the child's goodness will probably have little effect.

Let her know you approve when she spends
her time on something worthwhile.

Shaping is the word used to describe the gradual process of building up desirable behaviors by (1) structuring situations in such a way that the child can please you, (2) by rewarding good behaviors when they occur, and (3) by not paying attention to things you can't approve of.

Example:

DO: You want your 4-year-old to begin to dress himself. You tell him that you'd like him to put his clothes on in the morning and that he should try to get dressed by himself before he comes downstairs the next day. You can avoid having to bother him about putting on clothing that does not match by laying out the clothes he should put on the night before (structuring). Even if he puts his shirt on backwards, he has taken a step in the right direction by trying to dress himself, so you should reward him, perhaps by saying, "Oh, look, Bobby got dressed all by himself?" You can then put the shirt on frontwards for him with no comment about it.

DO NOT: Do not say, "Oh, you did it wrong; that's backwards." The child would feel that he hadn't satisfied you and would be less likely to want to try again than if you praised him and helped him to get the shirt on frontwards. It is best if you make no comment at that time, just casually help him.

Some Points to Remember About Shaping Behavior:

1. Make sure the child has the mental and physical ability to master the task so that he doesn't become frustrated by trying to do something that's too hard for him. (See What Parents Can Expect of Children, Lesson 1.)

2. It is important that the child know what you like and what you don't. You must have your goals straight in your own mind in order to let him know what is expected.

3. You must repeat your messages about what you like and don't like again and again. Saying something once is rarely enough.

4. You must not change the message. Be consistent in your reactions.

Punishment has its limits.

Many parents use punishment much more than approval because they don't know that there's a better way to teach children. The circle of disapproval and punishment is very unpleasant for parents and their children.

Some of the limitations of punishment are:

1. Children learn to avoid those people who punish them, and are less likely to go to their parents for help and love if the parents continually punish them.

2. Children may stop a behavior for which they are punished when the one who does the punishing is present, but may repeat the behavior when that person is not present.

3. The more a punishment is used, the less effective it becomes. Therefore, parents may find themselves using harsher and harsher punishments.
4. Parents who use physical punishments (like spanking) teach their children to use physical aggression too.
5. Punishment teaches the child what behaviors parents do *not* like, but structuring and clear instructions are needed to learn what they *do* like.

Example:

Your 15-year-old daughter is *required* to study a foreign language in high school. She hates the course, dislikes the teacher, has little talent for languages, and doesn't see when she will ever have any use for French anyway. So she refuses to study and gets punished. Perhaps you may send her to her room every night until her French is done, in spite of the fact that she claims she gets a headache when she tries to study French.

Punishment in this case would be a mistake because you would be adding one more negative element to an already negative situation, making the child even more resentful and less likely to study. In such a situation you might introduce some kind of

(Example continued on next page)

> *Example:* (Continued)
>
> positive element which really has very little to do with the behavior you want to promote. You might say, "Sandra, I know you hate to study French, but I thought maybe you would find it less bothersome if we kept a record of each day that you get your French done by 9 o'clock. Each time you do, you'll get a check mark on this chart, and for every five check marks you'll get to see a movie on Saturday night."

This is not bribery, as you might think, but a way of putting a positive element into a situation which holds only misery for the child, but which she should be helped to handle. Remember, the alternative is *failure*. Often, showing a child your pleasure may be enough to foster desired behaviors, but in some more extreme cases you may have to add an "artificial" positive element as described above.

When should you use punishment?

There are times when it's necessary to use punishment, but keep in mind that it must be used carefully and infrequently if you want it to have some effect. Listed below are times when punishment *might* be called for.

1. When a point must be made quickly because of safety, as when a child plays in the street.

2. When the problem behavior occurs so often that there is no good behavior to reinforce.

3. When reinforcement doesn't work because the child gets more pleasure from the problem behavior than from the reward (for example, stealing cookies).

SUMMARY

Creating an atmosphere of approval and reinforcement by rewarding and praising your child for good behaviors will make you and your child get along better than you would if you created an atmosphere of disapproval and punishment in your home.

●●●●●●●●●●●●●●●●

Please turn now to Practice Section 6, p. 137

7
RULES, LIMITS, AND CONSEQUENCES

Sometimes you must make rules or limits for your children to follow so that they can learn to behave in the ways you'd like. If children have too many rules to follow or if you punish them too harshly for breaking rules, they may learn to lie and be sneaky. If they have too few rules they won't know how to please you or themselves. This lesson discusses ways to make and enforce rules which will help children learn self-control and responsibility.

RULES, LIMITS AND CONSEQUENCES

What are limits?

Limits are rules that tell you when and where to stop. Broken limits are enforced with consequences.

Why should you use limits?
1. All of us need to know what the boundaries of our behavior should be. Within those boundaries we are free to make certain choices and decisions.

2. You can make it easier for children to control themselves and be responsible when you let them know how far they can go. You do this by stating clearly your rules, or limits, then enforcing them.
3. Limits are often necessary to protect the safety of children or others, and to protect valuable property.

When should you use limits?

It is often difficult for adults to know what limits to set on children's behavior. All children need to know that certain things are OK and others are not. If rules are too few or not clear, children will be confused and unable to learn how to please themselves or their parents. Setting reasonable limits and reasonable consequences for broken limits helps children to learn to be responsible for their actions.

The most important thing to remember when setting limits is to set only those which are important enough to you and your child to be enforced *every single time* they are broken. Don't make unnecessary limits which can't be enforced. If a child has too many limits to deal with, he will resent them, tend to ignore them, or learn to sneak around them.

Making Rules

Before you make a rule, ask yourself whether the rule is entirely necessary. Perhaps structuring, a parent message, or showing understanding will solve the problem. But if a rule does seem necessary, make sure it fits the situation, can be enforced, and is effective in preventing unwanted behaviors. A rule which is not suitable can sometimes be worse than no rule at all.

Example:

Michael, age 5, in spite of many threats and spankings, leaves the yard to play with other children whenever his mother's back is turned. She makes a rule that he must stay inside unless she or his father goes with him. As a result, he's inside most of the day, which is bad for both mother and son. Sometimes she gets so frustrated she lets him go out,

(Example continued on next page)

Example: (Continued)

thus breaking her own rule. Sometimes she punishes him for simple things more harshly than she should, because he is inside and getting on her nerves.

Michael's mother's rule is a very poor solution to their problem. A fence around the yard, a baby-sitter to go out with him, or rewards for staying put should work better.

But perhaps it's time for Michael's mother to realize that he's big enough to go out and play more on his own. Limiting him to his side of the street might be a better solution than trying to keep him in his own yard.

You can help your child to stay within the limits once they are made clear to him. Once the rules are set up, keep the following things in mind:

1. Repeat the rule many times if necessary. It takes children time to learn new behaviors. The child may want to test the rule to see if you will allow him to break it, or he may have trouble remembering the behavior you expect of him. Of course, younger children need to be reminded more often than older children because they have less experience and less self-control.

Example:

Billy, age 6, comes to the table with dirty hands for the 40th time, even though he has been reminded that he can't eat until he washes his hands.

Parent (firmly but calmly): "You must wash your hands before you eat." (A built in consequence exists here—the child doesn't eat until he washes his hands.)

ENDING I

Billy washes his hands.

Parent (pleased): "I'm glad your hands are washed—time to eat now!"

ENDING II

Billy: "My hands aren't dirty. I don't need to wash them."

Parent: "You don't see why you need to wash, but you must wash your hands before you eat." Parent doesn't let Billy eat until he washes his hands. Nothing more is said. No further consequences should be used. (For example, Billy would NOT have to miss his bedtime snack as a result of refusing to wash his hands).

ENDING III

Billy comes to the table with his hands washed after 40 previous failures to remember.

Parent (happily): "You fooled me—I was going to say, 'Wash your hands,' but you washed them already without me telling you. Great!

2. You can set up situations which make it easier for children to follow rules. (See *Structuring,* Lesson 5). First make sure the child knows exactly what you expect of him.

**Example*:*

"Sammy, your job is to take out the garbage. Dump it all into a plastic garbage bag, tie up the top, and put it in one of the garbage cans behind the house. Test to see that the lid is back on tightly."

---

3. When children *do* what you've asked, praise them for doing so. Don't ignore good behavior and focus only on bad behavior. You might praise them by saying things like, "How neat your room looks!" or, "Gee, it's really nice to see clean hands." If children know that you notice they are following the rules, they'll be more likely to *want* to follow them.

When children break the rules.

Sometimes even when you've structured the situation, reminded the child many times of what she should do, and rewarded her for good behavior, she still breaks the rules. At such times, try using a parent message like, "I am angry with you because I asked you three times this week to

Be sure that the child understands what
it is you are making limits about.

clean your room and you didn't do it. If it's not cleaned up by four o'clock, you can't go out to play this afternoon." If this warning fails to produce the desired behavior, you must enforce the *consequence* you've built in for broken limits. For example, the child would not be permitted to go out to play that afternoon, but must stay inside to clean.

The three kinds of consequences for broken limits are *natural consequences, logical consequences,* and *unrelated consequences.*

1. A *natural consequence* is one which simply follows as a direct result of a behavior, or one which you don't have to impose. For example, if a child throws his clothes around and refuses to hang them up, he'll have wrinkled clothes to wear. Or if a child comes in late to dinner, his food will be cold. Sometimes this kind of natural consequence is enough to cause children to change their behavior in the future.

    Of course, if the child doesn't care about eating a cold meal or wearing messy clothes, the parent must use some other kind of consequence. But parents shouldn't be afraid to let natural consequences take place *unless* they are destructive or dangerous. For example, you couldn't let a child experience the natural consequence of running out into traffic or of leaning too far out a second story window. But there are many other situations in which the natural consequence is neither destructive nor dangerous, like when a child refuses to eat his dinner one night and is hungry until it is time for his bedtime snack as a result.

2. *Logical consequences* are those which you must impose upon the child but which have a direct connection with the broken limit. For example, if a child leaves all of the tools he's borrowed from you lying around after he's been told several times to put them away, he loses his privilege to use the tools for several days. If a child leaves her bicycle in the street, you might impose the logical consequence that she can't ride her bicycle the next day. It is much easier for the child to make the connection between leaving her bike outside and not being allowed to ride it the following day, then it would be for her to make the connection between leaving the bike outside and an unrelated consequence like not being able to watch TV.

3. *Unrelated consequences* are those which you impose as a last resort when natural or logical consequences haven't worked. Even when using unrelated consequences, however, don't go overboard with the punishment. Remember that you are trying to teach the child to master a

behavior on his own, and that a punishment that is too harsh or hard to enforce may defeat your purpose. The child is likely to remember only the extreme punishment, *not* that he should follow the rule.

Children learn an important lesson by having consequences attached to their behavior. When they know for certain what is expected of them and what will happen when they don't follow the rules, they learn to take responsibility for their actions. They will remember that what happens to them as a result of their actions is under their control. For example, if a child knows that every time she makes a mess while painting pictures at the kitchen table, *she* will have to clean it up, she can choose either to be neat or to clean up the mess.

Here is an example which will help you to distinguish between natural, logical, and unrelated consequences:

Example:

John, age 9, leaves his catcher's mitt in the yard after being reminded to bring it inside to his room.

1. Natural consequences might be: it rains that night and the catcher's mitt is still wet when he wants to use it the next day, or that the dog takes it

(Example continued on next page)

Since the natural and logical consequences of breaking the rule are directly related to John's action, they are more likely to be effective than an unrelated consequence.

Some rules about making rules:

1. Rules should be stated positively, not negatively.

Examples:

Like This	*Not This*
Homework first, then T.V.	If you don't do your homework, you can't watch T.V.
Taste all the foods served, then you get dessert.	If you don't try a little of everything, you don't get dessert.

Exercise:

Change the rule below into a positive statement.

If you're not ready for bed by nine, I won't read you a story.

2. A rule should be spelled out in specific terms so that it can be enforced easily with no question about whether the child has followed it properly.

Examples:

Like This   *Not This*

Your clean clothes must be folded and put into the drawers or hung in the closet; dirty clothes go in the hamper.

You'd better take care of your clothes.

You must wash your face and hands, comb your hair and be dressed in clean clothes before going to school.

You must look neat before leaving for school.

Exercise:

Put the following rule into more specific terms.

I expect you to have all your work done properly.

3. If you have stated a rule several times and the child has not followed it even *after* several warnings, build in a consequence. The consequence should be appropriate to the broken limit. That is, it should be easy to apply, it should be one which you think will work, and it should be no stricter than is necessary to make the point. Make sure you impose the consequence every time the rule is broken, or the child will think it doesn't matter if the rule is broken.

Another important point to remember about a consequence is that it should be something that is not too hard for *you* to carry out. For example, the "wet glove" consequence would be a poor choice for you if you would feel obliged to replace it and could not afford to do so. *You* must be comfortable with the consequence. It is *always* possible to think of a different consequence.

Examples:

Like This	*Not This*
"You haven't finished your homework. Remember, TV after you finish." (Turn off TV or send child to another room.)	"You didn't finish your homework. No TV for a week." (This consequence is too severe.)
"If you track in mud, you'll have to clean it up." (See that child does so by a certain time.)	"If you track in mud, you'll never go out on a rainy day again." (This consequence has little meaning because you can't enforce it.)
"If you are late arriving home from Sunday School next week, you will have to stay in for the afternoon."	"If you don't get home from Sunday School on time, I'm not going to let you go any more." (This is not a good conquence because you would not want the child to miss the religious education.)

Note:

Don't fall into the trap of "getting the child to confess." If you are certain, or nearly certain, that your child broke a rule, *don't* say, "Maria, do you know who got the floor muddy?" This makes her think you might believe she's innocent and gives her a chance to say "the dog" or "Billy did it" to avoid having you get mad at her. Confront the child directly by saying, "Maria, please mop up the mud you tracked in." *If* you find out you were wrong about who did it, simply apologize with a parent message. This teaches a much better lesson than using the "third degree" to try to get the child to admit her mistake.

Exercise:

Write the following rule using a more appropriate consequence.

If you forget to close the door, I'm not going to let you in the house next time you come home.

The point of the exercise and examples above is that if a child breaks a rule and you have told him the consequence, you *must* follow through on imposing the consequence. Otherwise he will continue to test the rule to see if you will enforce it. That's why it's important *not* to make threats you can't or won't follow through on. Trying to "scare" a child into good behavior ("If you don't eat that spinach, you won't get any food for a week!" or "You'll stay home this weekend all by yourself while we go camping if you don't come in here.") is a very poor way to try to teach good behavior.

4. Let natural consequences follow a broken limit whenever possible.

Example:

You've explained to your six-year-old daughter that she will get hurt if she runs on the gravel. She continues to do so and skins her knee. The skinned knee makes a bigger impression on her than twenty threats or a slap.

---

5. When natural consequences don't work or don't apply, move on to a logical consequence.

Example:

Your child doesn't care about wearing messy clothes when he's left them lying around. You make a rule that the clothes must be put away or the child must iron them.

---

6. If the logical consequence doesn't work, move on to an unrelated consequence.

Example:

"You're still not picking up your clothes even though you've got to iron them, so you'll have to pay a penny fine each day for each piece that isn't picked up."

---

7. Whether the consequence is natural, logical or unrelated, it should be no bigger or more severe than necessary to make the point.

> *Example:*
>
> *Not* this: Your child, age 10, doesn't finish her homework before going out to play as you've told her she must. You impose the consequence that she must stay inside for a week. Instead of learning what you want her to learn ("I must do my homework right away before I go outside.") she feels angry and bitter, thinking, "All I did was not do my homework and I'm stuck inside for a week!"

If rules are too strict and consequences too severe, the child will learn to be sneaky and behave only in front of the people who punish her. He may even learn to lie to avoid punishment.

8. Make sure the child hasn't outgrown the need for the rule.

> *Example:*
>
> You have had a rule for a long time that your son is not allowed to cross streets on his bicycle. He is now eleven years old and able to cross a street safely. You should change the rule to allow him more independence and responsibility.

9. Don't be fooled into thinking that the thing which most hurts or scares the child is the best consequence to make him behave. It may work sometimes, but all too often it will cause resentment, anger, withdrawal, misbehavior elsewhere or a revolt against rules.

Example:

Robert's parents punish him for breaking rules by taking away the things he loves most. Once they even gave his dog away as a last resort to teach him to put his bike away. After a while Robert began to steal things he wanted from stores because he felt so frustrated about being punished so hard.

Some points to remember about limits:

1. Is making a rule the *best* way to solve the problem?
2. If so, decide what the rule should be.
3. State the rule clearly to the child so that she understands exactly what you expect.
4. If the child follows the rule, praise her for obeying.
5. If the child breaks the rule, remind her of it, giving her a chance to follow through on the reminder.
6. If she continually breaks the rule after many reminders, add an appropriate consequence.
7. Impose the consequence *every time* the child breaks the rule thereafter.

8. If the rule continues to be broken, take another look at it:

   a) Is the rule not clear, too harsh, or one that's too hard to enforce?

   b) Is the consequence suitable? Not too much? Or too little?

   c) Is the consequence always imposed?

   d) Use other skills such as parent messages and showing understanding to explore the problem with the child.

   e) Revise the plan and begin the process again, remembering the usefulness of reinforcement as well as limits.

SUMMARY

Rules and limits can help your child to learn responsible behavior when you: 1) state them clearly and positively, 2) when you don't impose too *many* rules, and 3) when the consequences are reasonable and consistently enforced.

●●●●●●●●●●●●●●●

Please turn now to Practice Section 7, p. 141

8
PUTTING IT ALL TOGETHER

Now that you have learned a number of different skills to help you establish a better relationship with your child, you may wonder exactly which one is likely to be best in a given situation. This lesson is designed to answer this question by providing certain guidelines to follow when you are deciding how to act with your child in different situations. The examples and exercises included here are intended to make you more aware of the elements in situations that are the most important ones and that deserve the most attention.

SELECTING THE PROPER RESPONSE

You have learned in previous lessons about listening to children and trying to put yourself in their place, and then responding to show that you understand their points of view (showing understanding). You have learned to tell them how *you* feel when your feelings are an important issue (parent messages). You have thought about how to take positive steps to set up situations and events so that children will find it easier to do the things they should do (structuring and reinforcement). You have explored the use of negative controls to direct children away from things which they should not do (limits). You have studied the best times to use each skill. Now we would like you to learn how to fit the proper response to any given situation.

Knowing when to use each response is just as critical as knowing how to use it. Using a particular response at the wrong time could be almost as bad as not knowing effective responses in the first place.

Example:

Just as it is wrong to laugh at a funeral, it is wrong to try to tickle a really sad child into laughing. Tickling him when he's unhappy amounts to denying his feelings. It's a little like putting a band-aid over a wound which will certainly require attention later. Perhaps the child feels better for the moment, and you might feel that your jollying him out of his troubles helped, but later he might wet the bed, get a "psychological bellyache," hide, or break or steal something as a result of his inner tension.

What is the child's point of view?

The first rule for every situation is: *What is the child's point of view?* How does he/she feel? What are his/her needs and goals? The more carefully you try to see things through his or her eyes, the more accurately you will be able to understand your child and respond appropriately. Even in situations where you can't allow the child's needs and wishes to take over, it is vital that you consider his/her point of view if you want the child to understand you and react appropriately.

Example:

Your eight-year-old daughter complains that she's not feeling well. She says she doesn't want to go to school. You take her temperature and decide she's faking because she has no fever. You send her to school. That night she breaks out in chicken pox. How would you feel? How would the child feel? Both of you would know that you were wrong. You would feel guilty and wish that you had a sure way of knowing when she was sick. Your daughter would lose some trust in your judgment. Several undesirable outcomes could result from your innocent mistake about the child's feelings (and health).

We often commit the same kinds of errors in other areas, making decisions that don't make sense to children. The less you make sense to them, the more likely it is that they will oppose you, either actively by openly defying you or passively, by "forgetting" what you expect of them. That's why it's critical for you to *consider the children's viewpoint* and *let them know* that you are doing so *even* when you can't let their feelings control the outcome.

Situations where the child's feelings can take top priority

Once you understand how the child views what is happening, you go on from there to decide how much you can allow the child's feelings to influence the situation. That will depend upon what is at stake.

Example:

Your child, age 7, gives you a gift which is not suitable for you. He's thrilled with himself for surprising you and for having gone to pick it out and pay for it all by himself. He thinks you'll be pleased with him because he's given you a nice thing. But this gift happens to be your third wallet, and an ugly, overpriced one at that. Here certain issues come to mind. What are you going to do with this

(Example continued on next page)

Example: (Continued)

wallet? How are you going to teach your child to spend money wisely? What can you say to the child about the gift he's given you? The following section will help you answer such questions.

Question:

In the above example, what should be your priority in making a response?

Answer:

The child's feelings should be given top priority in this situation for these reasons:

1. If you are negative about the gift or lecture on how to pick gifts, even in a kind way, you fail to take the child's viewpoint into account.

2. He will think that you don't appreciate his trying to please you.

3. You miss an important opportunity to reinforce or reward him for trying to do the right thing. He might come to the sad conclusion that he shouldn't give gifts so that he can avoid being criticized.

4. Your advice about how to give the *right* kinds of gifts probably would not sink in because the child would be feeling so disappointed.

In this situation the child's strong wish to please you is the most important issue. By giving it top priority, you honor his feelings and you reward the beginnings of the loving, giving kinds of behavior that you value.

Question:

What could you say to the child?

Answer:

You could say something like this when the child gives you the gift:

First response: "It really makes you happy to surprise me with a gift you picked out all by yourself." (showing understanding).

Second response: "I'm happy, too, that you want to please me for my birthday (parent message). I'm going to use this as a special wallet to keep your lunch money in" (structuring).

In this way you can positively reinforce his gift-giving efforts *first* and worry *later* about teaching him to spend a dollar wisely. Since he will have to buy many more things in the future, you will have many other chances to teach him what kind of things to buy without interfering with his feelings about giving gifts in order to please others.

It is often necessary to sort out your priorities like this when the issues involved in a situation are not clear-cut.

112

Example:

When you got home late one afternoon, your daughter, who'd never tried such a thing before, had prepared her own lunch. She was clearly proud of herself and thought you would be too, even though in her eight-year-old way she'd chosen strange foods and had made a little mess.

Question:

What might you say to your daughter?

Answer:

Keeping in mind that you should recognize the child's viewpoint and reinforce or reward desirable behaviors, you might respond as follows:

First response: "You made your own lunch. (Said with a pleased voice.) You really feel good when you do a grown-up thing like that. (Showing understanding.)

Second response: "I'm happy, too. (Parent message.) In fact, I'm so happy that I'm going to help you clean up." (Reinforcement.)

This approach would be effective in helping the child learn to be neat and sensible about making lunch. It would be more effective than if you gave top priority to your feeling that she chose weird food and made a mess, or that she should have waited until you got home. That would be discouraging to her. Helping her to clean the mess makes it clear to her that the cleaning should be done, without giving her the idea that the mess is more important to you than her efforts are. You will have many more chances to structure and reinforce lunch-making skills if you make her feel appreciated for being independent.

Situations where the child's feelings can't take top priority

You can't always give the child's feelings first consideration as in the preceding situations. Here are some examples of situations in which the child's viewpoint can't be considered the most important factor because higher priorities exist. You must, however, *recognize* the child's feelings even when you can't give top consideration to them.

Example:

Your child is angry. He was supposed to go to town with a neighbor to buy a game you had promised him. Then the neighbor decided she had no room for him in the car. He is now mistreating the dog, taking out his anger on the animal.

Sorting out the priorities here reveals that several issues are involved:

Issue One —   his feelings of disappointment and anger.

Issue Two —   your concern for the safety of the child and the dog.

Issue Three —   your own strong feelings about cruelty to animals.

Question:

Which issue takes priority here?

Answer:

You must stop the situation and *NOT* reinforce it in any way. You will have an opportunity to discuss his feelings when he calms down. Waiting may lead to either the boy or the dog being hurt.

Question:

What might you do and say?

Answer:

Here is one good way to deal with it:

Parent: (Going to the child and separating him from the dog, even against protests.) "Jimmy, you are really angry — so angry that you feel like beating up Frisky". (Showing understanding.)

Jimmy: "Yes, I wanted to go to town. I was promised."

Parent: "You'll have to leave Frisky alone, however. (Limit.) I know it's awful for you to miss your trip to town and I'm very sorry that it happened. (Parent message.) I'm trying to work out a time for a trip to town for you tomorrow with your Dad. (Structuring.)

Exercise:

Your child, age 5, wants to print her own Valentine cards. You are really rushed trying to get dinner ready. There's no way she can do it all by herself, since she is just learning to print.

1. What is the child's point of view?

2. What is your point of view?

3. What are other important issues to consider:

4. How would you respond? Give your first and second responses.

Example:

Your child was so happy to learn that he was going to receive a new bike for his birthday that he rushed out to promise to give his old one to his friend, whose parents can't afford to buy him one. Unknown to him, you had promised the bike to your sister, who needs one for your nephew and can't afford to buy one either.

Issue One —	your child's feelings of excitement and generosity.
Issue Two —	his friend's disappointment.
Issue Three —	your promise to your sister.
Issue Four —	her and your nephew's disappointment.

Questions:

How can you avoid ignoring your son's and his friend's feelings and still honor your own and your relatives' feelings?

What deserves top priority?

Answers:

Either way of giving the bike away will reinforce generosity. Since your promise to your sister was made before your son's to his friend, it would probably be best to honor it.

What might you say and do?

You could respond something like this:

Parent: "You can't wait! You're so excited about getting a new bike, and you'd like to share your happiness with your friend. (Showing understanding.) I hate to spoil your plans, Donny, but I promised the bike to Aunt Dorothy a long time ago when it was still a surprise that you'd be getting a new bike. She can't buy one for Billy. I really need to keep my promise." (Parent message.)

118

Donny would probably express disappointment and might be a little angry since he had things changed on him. You should continue to show him that you understand and accept them. Regardless of how Donny responds, you should share the job of telling his friend with him. You are partly responsible for things turning out as they have. Your son only wanted to be good to his friend and shouldn't have to bear the burden of breaking bad news alone. Of course, if he had known your plans, it would have been a very different situation.

SUMMARY

It is important that you use the skills you have learned at the right times to help your child learn to feel understood and to learn to do what he must to become a mature person. Ordering priorities about different points of view, and other issues will help you to do this. If the child's point of view can be top priority, then showing you understand him will probably be enough. If your viewpoint or some other viewpoint or issue must decide the outcome, then the child will need to deal with that. First you would try to use a parent message, and then perhaps a structuring or limiting response if the parent message doesn't do the job.

The goal of always trying to accept the child's viewpoint first will help you to come to better decisions about what really does deserve top priority. It will clarify for you and him where the child is coming from, give you a moment to consider where you are, and help the child realize that even if his point of view cannot decide the outcome, you, at least, have based your decision on a clear notion of what's going on. This is fair. Most children learn that things cannot (and should not) always come out exactly as they want them, but they do expect and *deserve* fairness. The problem-solving steps outlined in this lesson will help you to be fair to your child, yourself, and others.

●●●●●●●●●●●●●●●●

Please turn now to Practice Section 8, p. 143

Practice Section 1

CHILD PERFORMANCE ON DEVELOPMENTAL TASKS

Pick a child in your home, or that you know. Remember his/her behaviors.

1. List a few behaviors you think are below those expected for this child's age:

2. List a few behaviors that seem to be above this child's own age:

3. List a few behaviors which this child has had no opportunity to learn (or which you have not had a chance to observe because of limited opportunity) but which you think others his or her age might be able to do:

Practice Section 2

SHOWING UNDERSTANDING, PART ONE

I. Choose the word or words in the column on the left which describes the child's feelings in each of the situations on the right:

Feeling Words   *Situations*

angry

discouraged

proud

pleased

happy

sad

tired

frightened

1. Kathy, age 8, has surprised you by ironing her own blouse. She is feeling _____ .

2. Joe, age 10, slumps into a chair, near tears, saying "I didn't make the first-string team." He is feeling _____ .

3. Sandy, age 4, jumps back from the neighbors's dog, saying, "Tell the dog to go away." She is feeling _____ .

II. Choose the best response to the following statements.

"I just don't feel like eating right now." (Said by a child who's just discovered her dog is missing.)

    a) You're really worried that Rover won't come back.

b) It doesn't do any good to mope around, now come eat your dinner.

c) You know you should have tied him up when you left the yard.

III. Write a response showing understanding of the child's statement below.

"How come I always get all the dirty jobs to do around here?"

IV. Write your own response to each of the following situations, keeping in mind that you should let the child know that you recognize how he or she is feeling. Don't sympathize, criticize or give advice.

Situation A

Carolyn, age 9, comes home from school beaming. She holds up a certificate saying she won at the science fair.

Your response:

Situation B

Frank, age 7, comes home crying, saying, "Billy Martin took my baseball bat and won't give it back."

Your response:

Practice Section 3

SHOWING UNDERSTANDING, PART TWO

Five statements children make are listed on the next page. After each statement, write an answer which shows the child that you *understand and accept the feelings* in each situation. Keep in mind that you should not make suggestions, no matter how well-meant, nor should you criticize the child. After you have completed your answers, compare them to the preferred ones listed on the following pages.

Example:

Why don't I get to have a motorbike like all the other kids?

This: You're really disappointed that you can't have a motorbike.

Not this: All the other kids! You know only two boys who have them, and their parents are rich!

125

1. *Child Says:*

   There's nothing to do. All the other kids are playing kickball, and they say I'm too little to play.

   You say:

2. *Child says:*

   My new school is really neat. The teacher's really nice. She even gives lollipops to new kids who come into her class.

   You say:

126

3. *Child says:*

      Do you think that it really breaks your Mother's back if you walk on a crack? That is what Paula said when I walked on a crack.

    You say:

4. *Child says:*

      Listen to how I can play this song on the guitar. It took me only half an hour to learn it.

    You say:

5. *Child says:*

Would you walk past the Smith's house with me on the way to the store? Their dog always runs out and barks and jumps at me.

You say:

Suggested Responses for Items 1-5.

Any of the responses listed below are considered to show understanding of the child's feelings, when the right tone of voice is used. Compare them to those you wrote on the previous pages. Could yours be improved? Did you make suggestions or criticize the child in any of your replies?

1. If the child seems unable to find anything to do:

   "You're so bored because there's nothing to do."

   or

   If the child looks hurt:

   "It upsets you and hurts your feelings when the kids say you're too little to play."

   or

   If the child seems disappointed:

   "You really wanted to play and the kids just won't let you join in the fun."

2. "You're really excited about your new school."

   or

   "You like your new teacher."

3. If the child looks worried:

   "You're worried that you might hurt me if you step on cracks. And you don't want to.

or

If the child looks teasing:

> "It sounds like you're trying to tease me a little."
> (In this case, the question asked would not be a real
> question but rather a way of expressing an idea and
> a feeling; children often do that.)

4. If the child is beaming:
   > "You're proud of how fast you learned it."

   or

   If the child is fascinated with the actual playing:
   > "It makes you feel good when you know how to
   > play."

5. If the child is afraid:
   > "It's scary to go past there."

   or

   > "You're afraid that the dog might hurt you."

Practice Section 4

PARENT MESSAGES

Read each of the following situations. Think about what your feelings would be. Then write a parent message in the space provided. Remember that a good parent message is one which (1) clearly states your feelings to the child; (2) tells the child *why* you feel the way you do; and (3) does *not* accuse the child in any way.

Example:

You've had a hard day and you're trying to rest on the sofa. Your child, age 6, keeps climbing on you.

This:

I'm very tired and I want to rest. I must ask you not to climb on me now.

Not This:

You're always such a pest. Can't you see I'm trying to rest?

---

1. You're trying to get to the store before it closes. Your child (who must go with you) continues to play after being asked several times to put his jacket on.

   You say:

2. Two children are wrestling in the living room. You notice that they are getting wild and the younger one almost bangs his head on the corner of the coffee table.

   You say:

3. You have friends coming over to visit. You don't want your kids to make a lot of noise and run through the room while you're talking with your guests.

   You say:

132

Practice Section 5

STRUCTURING

We have talked about ways you and/or your child can plan ahead to avoid possible problems. Think of a problem which you have with your child which could be reduced or solved by structuring.

Example:

Your sons, six-year-old Dennis and eight-year-old Gary, fight constantly on long trips in the car. You are planning to take a two-hour drive to a camping spot next weekend. What can you do to prevent them from carrying on in the car?

You might provide a variety of things for them to do on the drive. A special new game to play in the car might help. You could ask each boy to choose a color, then to count the number of cars they see of that color. At the end of the drive the winner could be awarded a prize, but you could also award a "consolation prize" of equal value to the loser so that neither boy will be upset. This might give them an incentive to play the game rather than bother one another and you.

STRUCTURING

1. Write down a problem you have with your child.

2. State the way you'd like it to work out.

3. Decide what steps you can take to make things come out right by structuring for or with the child. List them here.

4. Sometime in the coming week, try out these steps with your child. After doing so, describe what you said and did here.

5. Did your structuring procedure work? How? If it didn't, write down what you think you could do to make it work next time.

Practice Section 6

REINFORCEMENT

We have discussed how a child responds to positive reinforcement by continuing or increasing those behaviors for which he is praised or rewarded.

Remember when you reinforce behavior to be specific about letting the child know exactly what you like. (See *Some Points to Remember About Shaping Behavior*, Lesson 6.)

Example:

Your child makes a drawing at nursery school and brings it home to show you. You admire it, saying, "Amy, how pretty; it's all blue!" Strangely enough, all of the drawings Amy brings home afterward are blue. *She* thinks that you liked the drawing only because it was blue, and failed to get the message you wanted her to get—that you liked the drawing because she did it herself. Your response is not "right" or "wrong;" it simply happens to confuse Amy. A less confusing response might be, "Amy, how pretty— and you did it all by yourself!"

1. Make a list of your child's behaviors which you would like to see increased. (Use the list from your lesson on Reinforcement if you like.)

    1.

    2.

    3.

4.

5.

2. Choose one of the behaviors you've listed to work on this week. Circle it. Is there some way you can structure situations so that your child is more likely to behave in ways you like? If so, how?

3. Each time the good behavior occurs, reward it. Keep track below of each time the behavior occurs and what you say or do to reinforce it.

Day and time behavior occurred.   How you reinforced it.

1.

2.

3.

4.

5.

Practice Section 7

RULES, LIMITS, & CONSEQUENCES

1. Think of one of the rules you have or ought to have for your child. Write it down. Explain why you need this rule.

2. Does your rule follow the guidelines we have discussed? If not, write the rule so that it does follow the guidelines. Remember that the rule should be stated positively and that it should be spelled out clearly.

3. What is the consequence for breaking this limit?

4. Is the consequence easy to enforce, suitable to the
   offense (not too harsh or too long-lasting), and one which
   you know can be effective? If not, change it so that it is.

Practice Section 8

SELECTING THE PROPER RESPONSE

Reminders

Keep the following points in mind when choosing the proper response:

1. Understand and take into account the child's viewpoint.
2. Identify the issues involved.
3. List all the issues, beginning with the child's viewpoint. Decide what takes priority. When ordering your priorities, be sure to consider the likelihood of the issues occurring again, thus giving you other, possibly better, opportunities for dealing with them.

Practice Situations

1. Your son, age 9, wants to ride his bike to a school friend's house. You don't usually approve of him going so far on his bike, even though you've never set limits about distance. Both you and your son want him to become more friendly with classmates, since there are no children of his age in the neighborhood.

1. The child's point of view:

2. Your point of view:

3. Other important issues to consider:

4. How would you respond? Give your first and second responses:

(Continued on next page)

2. Cindy, age 5, does not like soup or sandwiches, but will eat hot-dogs and canned spaghetti for lunch. You want her to try to like more foods, but you expect that when she gets a little older she will be more willing to try new things. Still, you get tired of giving her the same things all the time. She asks, "Mom, can I have hot-dogs for lunch again today?"

1. The child's point of view:

2. Your point of view:

3. Other important issues to consider:

4. How would you respond? Give your first and second responses:

(Continued on next page)

3. Your child, age 8, has been having a lot of nightmares lately. He wakes up the whole house and gets you upset. You know that he will be OK if he sleeps in a room with one of the other children, but you hesitate to give in on this. You feel he ought to be able to sleep alone. He says, "Mom, could I sleep in John's room. He wants me to and then I might sleep better?"

1. The child's point of view:

2. Your point of view:

3. Other important issues to consider:

4. How would you respond? Give your first and
   second responses:

(Continued on next page)

4. Tom, age 10, has been throwing snowballs at other children on the way to and from school. One of the neighbors and the school principal have called to complain to you about his behavior. You know that he has been having trouble with these children because they pick on him. You suspect that this may be why he is throwing snowballs.

1. The child's point of view:

2. Your point of view:

3. Other important issues to consider:

4. How would you respond? Give your first and second responses: